THE INTERNATIONAL EXECUTIVE

RICHARD LINDENMUTH

authorHOUSE®

AuthorHouse™
1663 Liberty Drive
Bloomington, IN 47403
www.authorhouse.com
Phone: 1 (800) 839-8640

© 2017 Richard Lindenmuth. All rights reserved.

No part of this book may be reproduced, stored in a retrieval system, or transmitted by any means without the written permission of the author.

Published by AuthorHouse 10/26/2017

ISBN: 978-1-5462-1320-8 (sc)
ISBN: 978-1-5462-1322-2 (hc)
ISBN: 978-1-5462-1321-5 (e)

Library of Congress Control Number: 2017916050

Print information available on the last page.

Any people depicted in stock imagery provided by Thinkstock are models, and such images are being used for illustrative purposes only. Certain stock imagery © Thinkstock.

This book is printed on acid-free paper.

Because of the dynamic nature of the Internet, any web addresses or links contained in this book may have changed since publication and may no longer be valid. The views expressed in this work are solely those of the author and do not necessarily reflect the views of the publisher, and the publisher hereby disclaims any responsibility for them.

Contents

Introduction vii
Chapter 1   Welcome/Bienvenidos 1
Chapter 2   Languages 9
Chapter 3   First International Assignment 15
Chapter 4   Settling In 20
Chapter 5   Problem Solving and Culture 31
Chapter 6   Travel Safety, Security and Protection 56
Chapter 7   A Local Guide 73
Chapter 8   Don't Bring Your Culture with You 80
Chapter 9   Financial Statements 85
Chapter 10 Review 89
Chapter 11 The Immediate Future 93

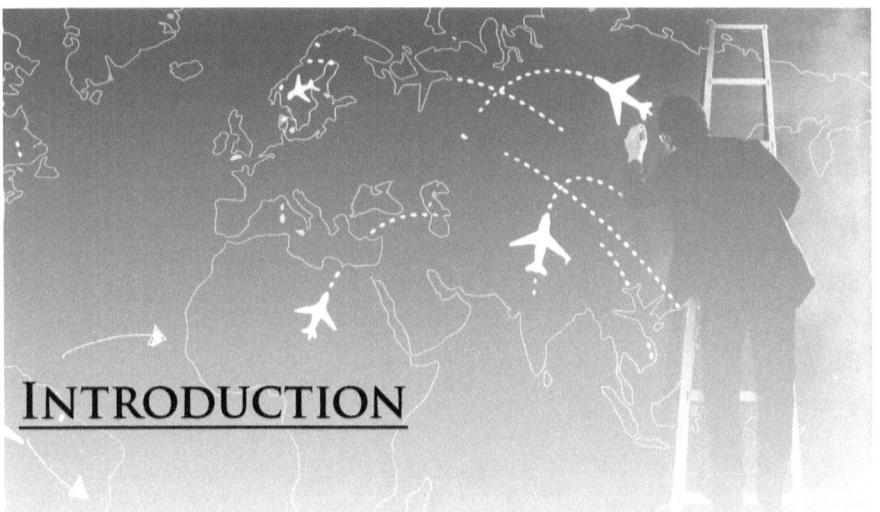

INTRODUCTION

Today business is global. Furniture and T-shirts are manufactured in China and Vietnam for consumers in the United States and Europe. Japanese tires are manufactured in the United States for distribution in Latin America. Grapes from Peru and Chile are shipped to the United States for sale in grocery chains.

Cultural differences in business discussions can lead to unexpected misunderstandings, which can range from humorous to costly.

This book is focused on the challenges faced in conducting business in different and/or mixed cultures. It is particularly aimed at the new manager who is developing a career and gaining global experience. There are also solid focal points

here for new and seasoned executives in the ever-changing global marketplace.

You would not go on a jungle safari without a knowledgeable guide. Why would you enter a new culture and attempt to conduct business without an experienced expert by your side?

As with learning a language, there are basic steps in learning cultural differences. The good news is that all cultures react positively when someone attempts to understand and adapt to that culture.

Adapting and adjusting business methods and listening in discussions is the path to global success.

"Life is either a daring adventure or nothing at all."
—Helen Keller

CHAPTER 1
Welcome/Bienvenidos

Working for a multinational company provides wonderful opportunities to travel and work outside of the United States. How do you get started working in that direction when the usual hindrance, similar to a catch-22, is that you need international experience in order to get a job overseas?

It certainly makes it easier to convince the international management team to send you overseas if you have lived and worked in several countries and speak several languages.

If you just finished college or completed your MBA, what are the chances that you have very much real international experience other than spring break in Cancun?

After spending several years traveling with the US Navy, including a tour in Italy where I learned to speak Italian, I went back to Wharton for an MBA and was ready for my first international assignment. Even then, Navy experience overseas was not considered true international experience.

Upon spending a great deal of time researching multinational companies, I found one well-known company with offices in just about every country of the world: The Singer Company (the sewing machine company).

Eventually I received an offer for a position in Singer's international treasury. My Uncle Bill, a C-level exec with Mobil Oil, gave me some wise advice. His advice was basically to choose the company well and to focus on doing a great job at the headquarters (HQ) first so that I became part of the HQ team.

He described his thought process: "If you move quickly overseas, the very first time that you call back to headquarters for support, money, advice, or anything else, the headquarters team will not even know who you are and certainly will not send you money without asking a lot of detailed questions."

His second piece of valuable advice was to get some financial background (not accounting) as quickly as practical. "You can always go from a finance position to marketing or general management, but you cannot go to a finance position from marketing."

When my parents retired and were moving into a retirement community, a new neighbor asked my father if he liked woodwork. My dad replied yes, and the new neighbor said, "Great, you're a freshman here, so I'll introduce you to the wood shop managers."

My dad commented that it seems like every four to six years throughout your life you are a freshman again and again.

When you are new to a company, you are a freshman again. Learn about the corporation. How does it make money? Map it out by country. Are the same products and services leading sales in each country? (This is usually not the case.) Learn about international operations. Read the financial statements and marketing information from the international offices that strike your interest. Learn about the management of each international operation, in the HQ as well as in every region and country. How does the money move around the globe? Where are investments being made? Who are considered to be the leaders in international operations? Read everything you can, just as if you were back in school. Listen carefully to the opinions of the senior international team at HQ.

Offer to work and provide support for projects in areas

that look interesting. Identify someone at headquarters who is involved in and leading international projects. There are usually some financial executives and marketing executives as well as the vice president of international and his or her team. Sales projects don't help much, but building a new factory, developing a manufacturing joint venture in Korea, and identifying potential strategic partners for entering the Brazilian market are the kinds of projects that build skills and relationships.

I suggest you find an advisor or mentor in headquarters. That person does not have to be leading the projects. More than likely, this is someone who has been there for a while and is respected by everyone for that one's knowledge and support. Ask for advice about your current job and how you can improve your expertise to support a move to the international side. Ask how to get more involved in international operations.

Nothing happens overnight, but if you are doing things right, you should get positive feedback for your interest and willingness to provide support.

Most international teams will visit headquarters a few times each year. Find out when these visits are taking place. Ask for introductions from your advisor or someone else directly involved with the visits. Don't be too pushy, and be sensitive to the short time available to the executive (sometimes including personal family vacation) when they visit from other countries.

If you are able to get an introduction, ask if there are meetings you could attend to learn. Many of these meetings are presentations of the financial, marketing, and country information from each operation. Private discussions between country management and CEOs or CFOs are just that and are done in private, but much of the information is shared with teams to keep everyone in the communications loop.

Your boss should not mind if you attend for a few hours, assuming you have been working hard and doing your regular job well.

Meeting the international team, listening to their presentations, and understanding some of their challenges allow you to get involved.

It is not a relationship if you meet, attend a meeting, and then say goodbye (adios) until the next meeting.

Perhaps you see a subject, risk, concern, or opportunity during the presentations (or dinner conversations) that interests you enough to pursue and becomes part of your continuing learning process. Tell someone on the team about your interest. The senior team leader (vice president, country manager) will be focused on conversations with the CEO and CFO and perhaps even board members. Find someone more junior (in age as well) and discuss your interest. Invite that person for a coffee. Use the word *invite* rather than saying, "I'll buy you a drink." Almost every culture in the world thinks an offer to buy a drink is very American and has no class. However, an invitation to get together at a local hotspot is hard to refuse.

Not every culture is open to inviting persons of other nationalities to be part of their team with full trust and open communications. It is important to begin developing these relationships slowly.

A quick personal note (today probably an e-mail, but not an e-blast) to the people that you met is the next step in developing a relationship. Connect on LinkedIn. After all, you are at the same company!

Out of sight is out of mind in any culture. Follow up with a short note on the areas in which you would like to continue to have some level of involvement. "How is the new training program at the factory going?" "If there is anything I can do here at headquarters to support you, please let me know." You have to be the judge about areas of common interest and the timing of follow-up notes to avoid being just plain annoying.

Anecdote: A Friend on the Inside

A general manager in Colombia placed an urgent request for $1 million due to a local government deadline for financial commitment to receive permits to build a new factory. It was Thursday, and the funds were needed by the next day. The probability that no one at world headquarters would even look at the request until Monday was high. He actually called and asked for "anyone" at the International Treasury to discuss the issue. When he was transferred to me, he remembered that I had talked with him about the new factory near Bogota. When I told him that I would try to help get the funding moving, he remembered that I sat next to him at a brief lunch and expressed interest in the expansion that was taking place in Colombia. We had also talked about the challenges in getting the proper permits for building and expansion. This brief conversation was right on the mark. He asked me to do everything I could to expedite the wire transfer and to assure that it was going to be there on time. The approved request for funding was indeed on a stack of things for Treasury to do on Monday. However, after I found the documentation and approvals and had a short discussion with my boss, the funds were transferred by wire before noon on Friday, and the factory construction was given all the government permits and approvals to move ahead. Although I had never worked in Colombia, I was now a solid member of their team at headquarters!

> "If you talk to a man in a language he understands, that goes to his head. If you talk to him in his own language, that goes to his heart."
> —Nelson Mandela

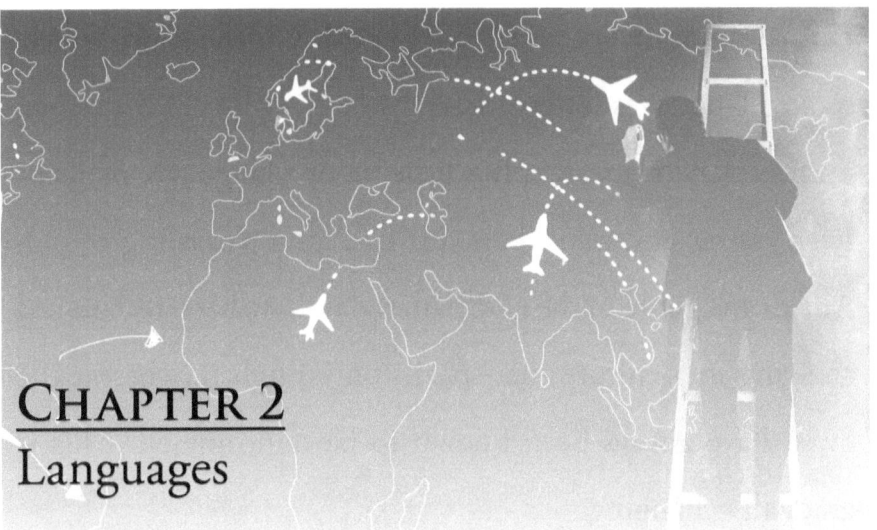

CHAPTER 2
Languages

If you are not interested in other languages, then why are you interested in international operations?

Language is the path to understanding the culture, values, and social etiquette in each country. It is important to understand what certain words mean in different cultures. This touches on a key point: It is not enough to just know the language, but you must understand the culture and how to use the language within that culture. It is important to understand how different cultures approach different social or business situations. Simply translating words from American English does not necessarily confer the same meaning intended.

Language is important but, in my opinion, there are only three major business languages in the world. Chinese,

Latin-American Spanish, and English are the most widely spoken languages for business.

It is okay to speak only a little bit of a language. *Bonjour*, *buon giorno*, and *ciao* all are just fine for a pleasant greeting. Americans, more in the past than today, have been recognized as living in a culture that speaks only English, whereas the Swiss have always been known to be multilingual. This is gradually changing.

My advice is that on the one hand it is nice to greet someone in their own language. However, in business the greeting implies that you are familiar with or have some basic knowledge of their language and culture. Since this takes much time and effort, it is more prudent to use your native language until they know you better.

Anecdote: Small Difference in Words, Big Difference in Meaning

There are many stories about Americans and language. My favorite is the one where an American executive is traveling with his wife to France. At a cocktail party he tries out his minimal French to introduce his wife to the French general manager. He proudly says *"Je voudrais vous introduire a ma femme,"* which has become a funny joke for the French. The correct way to say it is, *"Je voudrais vous presenter ma femme."* While "introduce" is fine in English, *introduire* in French means to "insert," or "put into," such as introducing or placing a chemical into a solution. You can see why the French often enjoy a great smile as introductions are made.

One additional comment about languages: It is often said that England and the United States are two countries separated by a common language. Yes, the words are English even though spelling (harbor, harbour) might slightly vary. However, in the everyday spoken language, meanings can be quite different between American and British English.

I traveled with a financial expert to review operations in Belgium, France, and Switzerland, with the last stop in London.

When we arrived, he said, "Finally, a country where I speak the language!"

I smiled and said, "Be careful! Not all words have the same meaning."

The local marketing manager, a proper British gentleman,

picked us up at the airport in his car. As we drove to the hotel, the conversation went something like this:

American: Do you have any hobbies?

Brit: Oh yes, I have a boat.

American: What kind is it?

Brit: It is quite a bird puller.

American: Oh, do you hunt?

Brit: Of course, I go out every weekend.

At this point, I had to stop the conversation and translate. I told the American that when the Brit said the boat was a "bird puller," it meant that it attracted girls (the Brit commented, "Of course!") and then I had to tell the Brit that the American surmised that he hunted ducks on his boat. We all had a laugh!

This is an important lesson to remember in project management. Even in the same culture, people often use the same words to mean completely different things. Don't assume that someone else understands your expectations just because you are both using the same words.

I often use the term *active listening*: Listening to what someone says and then repeating it back in your own words to confirm mutual understanding has serious value in global success.

Dr. Richard D. Lewis, in his book *When Cultures Collide* (1996), classified the differences in the culture of leadership by country. The classifications for styles of leadership numbered twenty-four and were reviewed by Cadreo.[1] It is worth a glance to better understand the large differences in leadership, even in countries that share the same language(s).

> The basic style categories defined by Lewis are as follows:
> American: Aggressive and focused above all on results
> German: Hierarchical but looks for consensus
> Asian: Consensus rules
> Latino and Arabic: Practices nepotism
> Indonesian: Autocratic, bases leadership on know-how
> Russian: Autocratic, trusts lieutenants, gets quick results, slow to implement
> Indian: Traditional and organized
> Norwegian: Led by bosses but friendly

---

[1] See http://www.cadreo.com/actualites/dt-les-24styles-de-management-dans-le-monde.

French: Autocratic and paternalistic, ignores middle management

Swedish: Democratic and decentralized

According to Dr. Lewis, these components do not evolve due to the heavy weight of history and tradition.

> "If you don't start you won't finish"
> —Croatian proverb

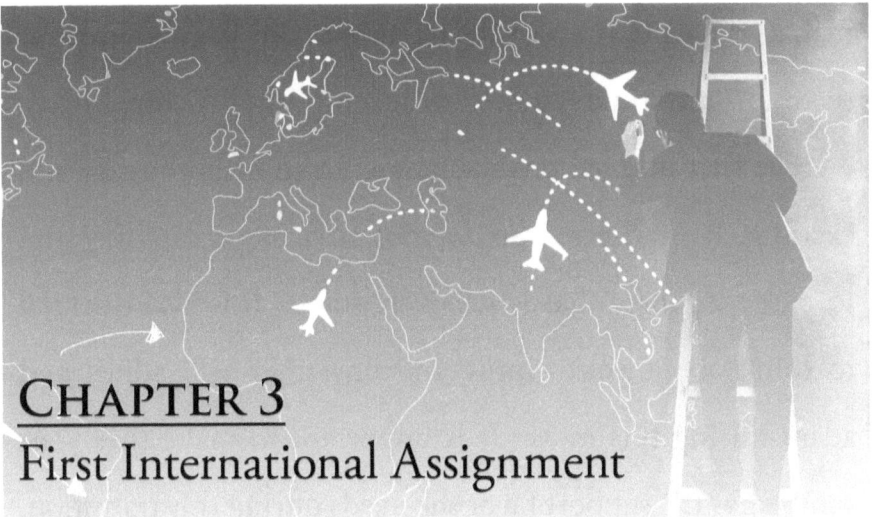

CHAPTER 3
First International Assignment

It takes time and effort to gain and then prepare correctly for an international assignment.

The first step is to do well at the company headquarters and to put together the basic foundation for an international assignment, including solid relationships and respect with key executives at the home office. This begins with doing a great job in your initial position while developing detailed information about international operations such as how the company makes money in each country. Is it in manufacturing and sales, marketing and sales, government business, and so on.

The next step is to develop relationships with the HQ international team and eventually the various country managements that visit HQ regularly. One year is probably the minimum time required to accomplish this correctly.

The first international assignment can be both scary and exciting. It is wise to choose your first move carefully and to pick a country that is relatively stable. It is also essential to think about your family and how they will adjust and adapt during this move. It is important to make sure your spouse has the support he or she needs during this transition. While the corporate structure will be similar to HQ, the new everyday tasks will be quite different.

My first international assignment was as a regional project manager for Africa and the Middle East based in Athens, Greece.

This chapter presents an overall picture of adapting with your family to your first international assignment.

Kali mera sas? Good morning. Wake up, you are in Athens.

Athens is your corporate regional headquarters for Africa and the Middle East. It used to be in Beirut, but when Lebanon became a war zone, many companies moved their regional operations to Athens.

The local laws provide regional headquarters with permits for residency. There are also no taxes for regional headquarters that conduct no actual sales or manufacturing business in Greece but create administrative and marketing jobs to focus on regions such as Africa and the Middle East.

Greece has a lot of amenities that translate well from American culture. There are good international schools. There is a modest international community with an American enclave. The hospitals are good, the US Embassy is helpful, and it has a magical blend of Eastern and Western cultures. Many Greek executives were educated in Europe or the United States.

English is widely spoken, the food is largely within the parameters of a normal American diet (goat cheese, olives, and retsina add a little zest!), and personal safety is similar to most US cities.

On your first day on the job, the first thing you do is meet the boss, Jean Marc. He was the one that you met with at HQ while you were working there. You were interested in the Greek international office, so you attended a meeting when the management group came to HQ. You got to meet the team and started building a relationship. When Jean had an issue, he asked you for help, and you quickly helped him secure what he needed from HQ. So when HQ encouraged him to start your international experience, he was more than willing to do so.

Jean Marc is from Brussels. (I've made up names and nationalities as a "representative" office.) His children go to a university there, and he and his wife travel back and forth often.

When you arrive at the office for your first day, Jean Marc introduces you to the financial controller, Alex, who is a Greek from one of the islands. He then introduces you to the marketing manager, Harry, who is from Great Britain. He and his wife live in Kifissia (a suburb), and their children attend the British school.

The sales manager, Faisal, is next. He is from Palestine. He speaks English, French, and Arabic. He and his family also live in Kifissia while their children attend the international school nearby.

Jean Marc shows you to your new office and introduces you to Fofi, your new admin and support person. She went to high school in Canada and just returned to Greece to get married.

Wow, talk about a cultural melting pot!

The office mission is to grow the business in Africa and

the Middle East. Everyone's job requires frequent travel to all of the countries in the region with all of the Greek business being the responsibility of the separate local Greek company that has 100 percent Greek management and employees.

> "It is not the strongest of the species that survives, nor the most intelligent.
> It is the one that is most adaptable to change."
> —Charles Darwin

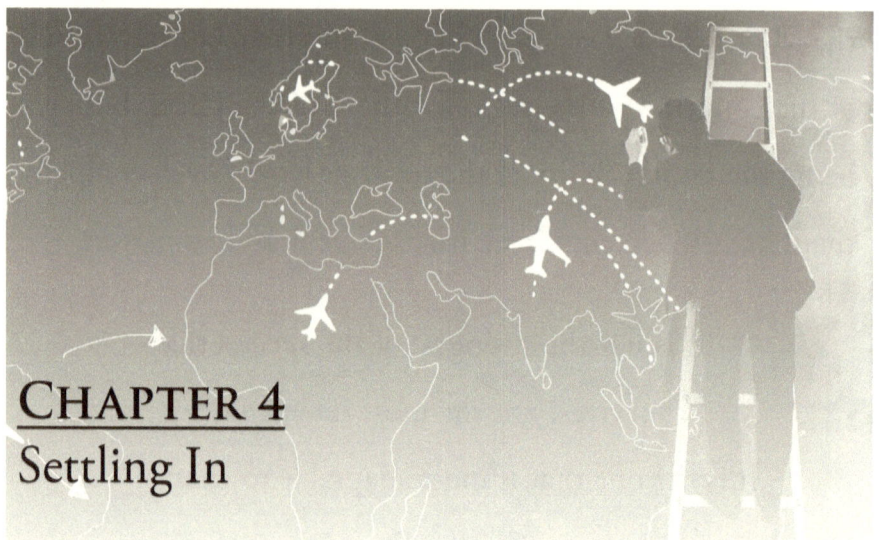

CHAPTER 4
Settling In

You knew about the assignment for two months prior to making the move to Athens. The company suggested (and you accepted) a two-week total immersion course in Greek for you and your wife. The Greek teachers provided insights into the language, culture, etiquette, and other critical issues for survival. You and your wife even went out for a few Greek dinners.

When we did it, the instructors greeted us with "*Kali mera sas* (good morning) every day when we arrived for lessons. We would have some Greek coffee, *metrio* (medium sugar) before class would start. We learned the basics of the language, including the use of familiar terms for family, children and close friends. (*Thee* and *thou* are no longer used in American English, but their functional equivalents are very much a part of other languages.) *Ti kanete?* How are you? in formal terms is generally used when speaking with others.

When we went to lunches and dinners, we learned how to order Greek food, and we also practiced using our fork in our left hand while keeping our knife in our right hand instead of constantly changing them as is common in the United States.

Your company had international movers come to your home and carefully pack and crate your furniture and goods for the international move.

The company nurse gave you a list of all of the vaccinations required for you and the family and made sure that you were up-to-date with things like hepatitis inoculations since you were traveling to developing countries.

The company would provide an automobile and subsidize the rent for an apartment or house. (This varies by country.)

Our company installed us in the Megali Britania. It is a wonderful hotel on Syntagma Square, which is the main square in the city of Athens. The Greek parliament building is right next to the hotel, and we could watch the changing of the guard from our hotel room window.

The hotel is a five-star hotel with great food and great

service. There is even a string quartet that plays classical music in the foyer prior to dinner in the evening.

It is challenging for a young child to sit through three meals a day in a hotel dining room, so the staff would invite our son, Michael, to go into the kitchen, watch TV, and have a Coca-Cola, which made it relaxing for everyone.

Wives and Family

The manager-executive has roughly the same environment that he did back home. Communications are in English. Business discussions are with many of the same people at headquarters. (This is why you spent your first assignment at HQ.) The products and services are exactly the same. In short, the initial changes for the executive are small.

It is exactly the opposite for the family. The family, particularly the spouse, has to deal with the local economy and culture from the very first day. English is not always spoken fluently in the local grocery store. Bargaining for goods is a normal part of the culture. "Oh, this is beautiful, but much too expensive for me" is polite and important. Not all goods are subject to bargain. However, it is considered naïve to simply pay the asked price for anything.

While you are being introduced to the company, the international wives, organized by Jean Marc's wife, Marie Claire, gather with your wife and talk about where to live, where to shop, areas of caution, security, schools, and basically commiserate that their husbands are always traveling and sometimes home only on weekends. This support group is important and multicultural. Your wife and family need some guidance to live in the new culture and business environment, and this local support group will provide a solid base since they went through the same things themselves.

Anecdote: Butchery Costs Extra

My wife came home from her first visit to the local market in Kifissia. She told me that she was not going to buy a live chicken and come home and kill it! Fortunately, I was able to tell her that there was a local supermarket where the prices were a little higher, but no chicken killing was required!

Driving the children to school, parking, shopping, haircuts, electricians, plumbers, and furnace experts all require a total immersion of your spouse and family in the local culture.

In some countries, this can be a significant issue. Greece is a great introduction to the blend of East and West and is generally one of the more friendly countries for international families.

Another thing to be aware of is that not only is the culture different, but the technology can be quite different as well. America is one of the more technologically advanced nations. Many times you will be shocked at the culture difference that is caused by a lack of or different technologies. Many countries are catching up or upgrading their infrastructure, but they may not know how to use it, or understand all the details of a newly installed technology. In my case, we were on a waiting list for one year for a home telephone.

Anecdote: Taking Children Abroad

In Morocco, we were invited as a family to have a nice dinner in the home of the country general manager for the Singer Sewing Machine Company.

My son Michael was seven years old. He had been to school

in Greece and Lebanon, and was going to the international school in Casablanca soon.

The dinner was wonderful. The lady of the house had a cook and a maid. When a plate needed changing or a glass needed refreshing, she had a small crystal bell that she would ring and the maid would come to the table to see what was needed.

Michael asked if he could ring the bell, and the answer, of course was yes. He rang the bell, the maid appeared, he asked for more Coca-Cola, and after the maid filled his glass, he turned to me and said, "Dad, we have to get Mom one of these bells!"

Michael was about the same age when we returned to the United States to visit his Grandma. He followed her around for hours until she asked if he watched TV. Where we were living at the time, TV was available only starting at dinner time until 11:00 p.m., and it was mostly news and adult programing. When he said no, she sat him down in front of the TV and turned on *Sesame Street*, which he watched for hours. The next morning, when I woke up at 6:00 a.m., I found Michael in front of the TV watching the farm report.

When I asked what he was up to, he said that Sesame Street would be on this channel any minute.

Anecdote: Playing with Fire

One night, when I told my landlord that I believed the furnace was running out of fuel, he grabbed a pack of matches and said, "Let's go look." Gas furnaces were new in Greece, and my landlord probably had never even refueled a furnace. This landlord had always had fireplace heating or space heaters, so he wasn't aware how dangerous using matches would have been. My first response to him was: "Give me twenty minutes in order to get my family to Athens, the next city over." Fortunately I talked him out of using matches and had brought a flashlight with me.

A new car has been ordered from Great Britain. After roughly thirty days in Greece, you receive notice that your furniture and household goods have arrived at the port. The real estate people and the executives' wives have been escorting your family to the various areas where international families live, and your wife has found "the place." It is the full downstairs of a brand new house with a Greek owner, and his family living upstairs. The house is great. It even has a fireplace.

Your automobile will arrive in two weeks, but in the meantime, rental cars are available.

The household goods seem to be delayed at the port. Alex, the controller, suggests that you visit the port, inspect your goods, and see if they can be expedited.

The customs officer responsible for clearing your household effects walks you and Alex out to the container and several large cartons encased in plywood, one of which seems to show signs of having been very wet.

You ask the customs officer when your goods will be cleared to move to your new house. He points to the many containers and crates in the yard and says that it will be several weeks before the goods can be cleared through customs and shipped to your new residence. After you express some concern that everything is out in the open and that you would really appreciate it if he could help you to make it happen faster, the official just nods his head and smiles.

At this point Alex calls you to the side and suggests that you give a tip to the customs official. You are a little concerned that this might not be a good thing to do. Alex suggests fifty dollars, or the wait for your household effects could be longer.

Alex explains how to do it correctly: You take out your passport, enclose fifty dollars, and hand it to the official, asking, "Can we move it a little faster, *parakalo* (please)?" The officer looks at the passport, the fifty dollars magically disappears into his pocket, and he agrees that the goods could actually move tomorrow, for which you say *efharisto* (thank you).

Alex assures you that a small tip to expedite something that the officer is going to do anyway does not break any rules. It is clear in this case that nothing would have cleared customs without the small tip.

Welcome to Athens! It is also not considered wrong or unethical by American rules as long as it is a small tip for something that the official would do anyway.

What is considered ethical is notably different in different countries. In many countries, especially Third World countries, small tips, what we would consider bribes, are the norm in business and keep operations running smoothly. However, it is important to understand the correct procedure for offering the tip. Just as with the case of putting fifty dollars in the passport, it is important to talk to a local business expert to understand the correct way to handle these exchanges. There is a big difference between tipping to make the process run smother and offering a bribe to get special treatment. If you think this is too unethical for you, realize that many cultures find it crazy that we tip our waiters for doing a good job, or tip the taxi driver for driving us someplace.

After I tipped the officer, I left with Alex and confirmed with the moving company that they could pick up the goods the next morning and deliver them to our new residence.

When the goods arrive, you discover that the one crate was indeed wet and everything inside it has water damage. Not to worry—the insurance rep for the moving company will be there tomorrow. You may expect to have to deal with a huge discussion about value and extent of the damage. This is not the Unites States.

The insurance rep turns out to be working for you. He suggests that your wife go out and shop to replace whatever she wants, and he will approve it against the insurance. Wow, new furniture. This is a great move.

Move-in day is successful. Alex's wife makes sure that there are no translation issues and things go smoothly.

"If I had an hour to solve a problem, I'd spend fifty-five minutes thinking about the problem and five minutes thinking about solutions."

—Albert Einstein

CHAPTER 5
Problem Solving and Culture

Greece is a good first move. It is not likely that you will move to a well-established country in Europe since they are likely to have entirely local management (with the occasional exception of a CFO or financial controller).

It is also not likely that your first assignment will drop you in a war zone or some similarly challenging business climate.

I was lucky at the Wharton Graduate School to have a professor of international business, Dr. Howard Perlmutter, who provided a two-day seminar with actual demonstrations of cultural differences in solving problems. It turned out to be a lesson that kept me out of trouble many times when I understood these basic differences.

The seminar included several cultural groups: Japanese,

French, German, American, and a mixed group that included representatives from each culture.

The task that was given to each cultural group to solve was a standard business problem. It was basically to introduce a new consumer goods product into the global markets. The product was an extension of an existing product line with additional functions and higher value. Launching the product required plans for pricing, beginning inventory, aligning sales and marketing programs, and building off of the current successful sales programs in the global markets.

The Japanese Approach

The first group to be given the problem in the seminar while we all observed was a group of Japanese businessmen. It was good to start with this group since their approach to problem solving is unique compared to the American and European approaches.

Each group was brought into the room and asked to take seats at a rectangular conference table.

The observers at this point watched the Japanese team enter the room. The most senior executive sat at the head of the table, followed by the next most senior executive to his right, and so it went around the table until the most junior Japanese executive was seated last.

The senior executive at the head of the table began by describing the problem, and he suggested a basic approach in a manner that allowed for no disagreement from any other member of the team.

The second most senior team member, directly to the right of the first speaker, then responded: "Yes, sir, you are correct. However, perhaps we should also consider…" and then went on to add another basic but important aspect of the problem and a non-controversial approach to solving it.

This continued around the table from the most senior executive to the most junior, and discussions continued until a solution was reached. The most senior executive summarized the problem and the solution for everyone.

The observers were American, French, Japanese, German, British, and Russian. It was interesting to see the reactions to this approach.

No discussion was permitted at this moment. The professor simply described the approach to problem solving to make sure that each of us agreed that we observed the same things.

The French Approach

When the French group entered the room, we were all ready to see if there was any special approach to seating. There was none other than respect for the most senior team members, allowing them to select seats first.

The same presentation of the problem was made to all groups, and many of the questions for clarification were the same for all groups as well.

The French group's approach was much different. One of the senior team members suggested that they should first describe the history of the problem before addressing the specifics.

The French group spent quite a bit of time describing the history. They began with discussions about how long the company had been operating and selling in this particular country and what the initial product line was when they opened the market.

There was quite a bit of interaction between team members, and everyone was respectful of each other's contributions.

The focus of the discussion moved to the current state of the problem, but not until after a description of the history of the problem was agreed upon. The solutions generally related back to the historical base and were consistent with those approaches that had been successful in the past.

The team leader (not the eldest, but the person who had the most experience with these products) provided the summary and conclusions for the observers.

The solutions that were eventually provided by the all of the cultural groups were similar.

The professor asked whether the history was important to solving the problem.

The answer from every French team member was: "Of course. How can you solve a problem unless you understand the history?"

The French approach was not as autocratic as the Japanese. There was much more interaction and discussion around and across the table.

It was clearly important for the French team to delineate the history of the products in the market and what changes had occurred over time. The French said that they needed to spend time establishing a clear history of the products and markets in order to establish a clear foundation for a successful product launch.

The French, unlike the Japanese, would politely interrupt one another to interject a thought, comment, or idea.

As an American observer, I could easily understand the approach although the initial lengthy focus on history seemed to waste a great deal of time.

The German Approach

The next group was German. They entered the room and were quickly seated at the table as the problem was presented. They asked similar questions for clarification and then began their approach.

The Germans began by focusing on the definition of the problem. Their approach was to establish as much precision as possible to assure that the foundation for their solution was solid. There was a great deal of detailed description of products, markets, demographics, and logistics for resolving the problems.

Once this foundation was established, the focus moved on to the final resolution. The team member that had the most experience in the introduction of new products made the final presentation of the summary and conclusions.

The professor asked, "Is it important in developing the solution to spend time discussing the description of the problem in such great detail?"

The German response was uniform. "Yes, how can you solve a problem unless everyone agrees on the details right from the beginning?"

The American Approach

The next group to address the problem was the American group. They entered the room and were quickly seated at the table. There was no visible order to the seating.

Once the problem was presented and the responses to the same questions for clarification were completed, the Americans began their approach to problem solving.

The Americans jumped right in and started talking about the desired results. There was quite a bit of discussion with two or three people talking at the same time along with some mild disagreements that were quickly settled (or ignored). For example, one team member suggested discount coupons. Everyone groaned and one fellow said, "No way for a new product launch with more product utility and value!"

The Americans worked backward from the desired results to develop the steps necessary for achieving those results.

Once a step-by-step approach to the problem was developed, they all agreed the problem was solved.

There were a few looks around the table and one person jumped in with a rough presentation of the summary and conclusions based on the step-by-step solution. Every American team member added a few comments during the presentation.

The professor asked, "Do you need to spend any time on the details or background to solve the problem?" The response from everyone on the team was that details would be addressed in the final action plan and that no additional background was required.

The Multicultural Approach

The next group was multicultural, with three members from each of the Japanese, French, German, and American teams participating in the final team approach.

The same presentation of the problem was made since these team members did not participate in nor observe the previous single-culture teams and their discussions. Some questions for clarification were asked and answered quickly. It was clear that some would have appreciated more time to ask detailed questions.

There was no particular leader, so one of the Americans jumped in, defining the expected results. A French team member suggested that the team needed to understand the history of the problem and opportunity before they could focus on the solution. There was no agreement on that approach. One of the Germans suggested that more detail was required to arrive at a solid solution, so the discussion focused for a short time on a few details.

The Americans dominated much of the discussion. The French expressed frustration with not being able to establish a foundation solid enough to approach the final solution. The Germans were a little pushier and got the discussion focused on product and logistic details for a moment or two.

The Japanese were absolutely quiet except for a few yes responses (*hai dozo!*). The end result was a basic and underdeveloped approach to a solution for the problem.

The professor asked if there were any major issues that were not fully addressed and needed more work.

Everyone expressed frustration. The French said, "Clearly more attention needs to be paid to history, establishing a foundation for the solution." The Germans responded that not enough attention was focused on the details required to develop a solution. The Americans said that the team needed to understand that the only thing that really counted was the result. The Japanese said that it was interesting and that everything was fine.

Overview and Observations

The final solutions developed by each group, with the exception of the mixed cultural group, were almost identical. There were perhaps one or two additions (more detail, more history, and so on) from each group. However, the final solutions would have been easy to implement by any of the teams present. Interesting!

The single-culture approach was much more team-participation based. It also followed the accepted and learned approach to that culture's way of problem solving, validated and held together by years of tradition.

There were comments by the observers that Americans

were much less respectful of each other in the discussions. This included comments that the Americans tended to jump to the results first, without developing a foundation for the final solution. In the multicultural team, the Americans were perceived as rude.

It is absolutely required that an international executive be sensitive to cultural differences in solving problems.

As you can see from this example, when a group from different cultures is poorly managed, the result is much worse than if the group is from a single culture. However, I have learned over my career that if the diverse group is well managed, the results are often better than any of the of single-culture groups. This happens because every culture has different perspectives and different ways of solving problems, all of which work, but when you combine them together in a well-managed group, you can build on each culture's strengths and create an even better solution.

Richard Lindenmuth

Problem Solving Lessons for the International Executive

The most important aspect of reaching a solution with other international executives and cultures is the process. Listening and observing is critical for understanding and deriving value from process. There is a good chance that bright people focused on solving the same issue will arrive at a similar conclusion.

There are also times when group members from different cultures do not agree on one solution. The signs and communications vary by culture for delaying, breaking off discussion, or simply agreeing that no deal can be reached.

Some cultures do not allow for an absolute *no*. Active listening is required to understand when there exists a slowdown in discussions or negotiations, or a gap in understanding that results in a lack of interest in pursuing the project any further. This direction may also come from someone senior in the organization who is not participating directly in the discussion, but receiving updates and providing direction from behind the scenes.

Many American executives have departed Japan after a

week of business meetings and dinners, thinking they had made a deal, only to discover that while the responses to the American questions were yes, they really meant, "Yes, we will continue to think about this."

Active Listening

Active listening is defined by Wikipedia as "a communication technique that requires the listener to feedback what they hear to the speaker, by way of restating or paraphrasing what they have heard in their own words, to confirm what they have heard and moreover, to confirm the understanding of both parties."

Active listening is a valuable tool for all international executives, valuable in many situations. However, it is an absolute requirement when you are in a multicultural and multilingual environment.

Everyone in your work environment can provide guidance for success if you just listen. Active listening is a tool that saves any serious misunderstanding due to cultural and language differences.

Americans are often accused of simply waiting until the

other person finishes a statement so that they can begin talking.

Anecdote: An Unfamiliar Ritual

I had the pleasure of installing a new factory manager in Malaysia. He had spent several years at the company's main factory. He had a Wharton MBA, and he spoke reasonable Spanish. He had enjoyed a study abroad program in Spain in his undergraduate days.

I flew with him from New York to Kuala Lumpur and spent several days with him, introducing him to the local management and employees. When we walked around the factory floor, he soon saw some process areas where improvements could be made.

I suggested that he go slowly, that he take a month to discuss the current processes with local management, walk on the factory floor to get a better understanding of how the people interact, and learn a little more about the culture.

I went on to Singapore the next day, intending to return to Kuala Lumpur within ten days.

Three days later, I received a call from one of our local

partners saying that I needed to come back quickly because the employees were going to walk out.

I got on an airplane, and three hours later I was at the factory. I asked the new plant manager to give me his thoughts on what was going on.

"One of the factory ladies believes that the factory has demons and is possessed. I told them all to go back to work, and there seems to be some disruption."

I explained to him that if someone believes that there are demons in the factory, there are demons. It is our job to "cleanse" the factory of demons so that things can get back to normal. He looked at me like I was a little off the mark, but he said that he would learn by actively participating in whatever needed to be done.

I learned this myself in similar but different situations in Indonesia and in Egypt.

In Indonesia, several workers believed demons were invading our operations. We got a village necromancer and held a ceremony where everyone dressed in traditional costumes. Each of the corners of the buildings was "blessed" and a bowl of rice was used to mark the areas. After the ceremony, everyone was relieved that the demons had vanished.

In Egypt we had some snakes in the trees of the garden in the middle of the factory area. In this case an expert was called in to eliminate the snakes. Instead of extermination tools, the expert brought a flute. I was simply amazed when he played the flute and a snake came right out of the tree and into a sack that he had prepared to carry the snake away.

I sought the advice of the local partner. We brought in a shaman.

We told him what the issues were. He talked with the factory ladies and then returned to give us a briefing on what needed to be done and how he would approach this critical issue. He performed a small ceremony with several of the factory ladies along with the new plant manager, who, after some discussion, agreed to wear a locally embroidered shirt for the ceremony.

The shaman, as part of a nice ceremony, pasted fresh rice on the forehead of the ladies and the plant manager. They then walked around the inside of the factory with incense and placed ceremonial bowls in strategic corners. There were a number of prayers and blessings given.

After the ceremony, the shaman declared that all demons were gone. Everyone returned to work with a smile.

I had a long chat with the new plant manager, restating that he needed to proceed slowly and occasionally ask the counsel of our local partner when something occurred that he did not understand.

He was a bright and successful plant manager who stayed at this plant for over three years, being recognized for his good management and productivity improvements several times by headquarters. He also participated in similar ceremonies in other countries throughout his long and successful international career.

Today, he is also a very active listener!

Active listening is more important when the basic language and culture are not your native language and culture.

Legal Changes and Problem Solving

In many countries (Nigeria, Tunisia, and Algeria, to name a few) the ability to own or continue to own 100 percent of a subsidiary, branch, or company has evolved to require partners at various levels. In fact, today the United States is one of a few countries where a non-US citizen or company can purchase 100 percent of the equity of a US company (with the exception of defense or national security companies and products). There are a few restrictions when it comes to infrastructure (such as telecom and utilities) where damage to the infrastructure would hurt US security. Smithfield Ham in North Carolina, for example, is now owned 100 percent by Chinese business people, as is Lenovo.

Basically, in today's global markets it is best to have a solid local strategic partner!

Anecdote: The Value of Local Partners

In Morocco, I was asked to find a new local partner to meet these legal requirements.

Morocco was going through a period of "Moroccanization." Companies needed a local partner to own 51 percent of the business. I was charged with locating a suitable partner and negotiating an agreement for the purchase of 51 percent of the company.

Eventually, we were approached by one of the prominent local families in Casablanca that expressed an interest in being partners.

The discussions began in a social manner. Getting to

know one another better before becoming partners was quite important.

I was actively listening to the discussions, which were mostly in French. There were two reasons for this approach. First, active listening always leads to better results. Second, I spoke reasonable French, although I had never negotiated anything more than a rug at the bazaar in French, and I was extremely fearful of making a mistake due to a simple language error.

As an active listener, I would slow the discussions, repeat in different words what I thought I had heard, and summarize where we were in the discussions.

It was a tedious process for everyone, and I often suggested a recess before moving on to the next subject or the next phase of the discussions.

The negotiations were completed successfully and everyone was happy with the results. Headquarters gave me a plaque in recognition of this success.

One year later, I had a discussion with the son of the new partner in Morocco. The son was part of every phase of negotiations and ultimately became the president of the local company.

He said that he remembered what a tough negotiator I had been during the discussions. He said that I repeated everything back to them several times and that at tense moments I would suggest that we take a break for an hour or get back together the next day.

What I did not tell him was that I repeated everything back to make sure that I understood everything in French and that we could keep everyone on the same page. I also did not confess that the real reason for the break was so that I could carefully review everything that had been said to make absolutely sure that I understood everything and also to make sure that I could carefully select the words (in French) for my response.

One lesson that I learned from this is that I now approach all negotiations in a similar fashion, even if the discussions are in American English.

An additional cultural area is legal practices. We often assume that since the way we are used to is the way something is done in our country and is a practical approach, that is the way it is done everywhere. We have all heard the admonition to never *assume* lest you make an "*ass* of *u* and *me*."

One example of a legal accounting practice is that in

Morocco (as in other countries in this geographical area) you are only required to have an opening balance at the beginning of the year and a closing balance at the end of the year for your legal books and accounts.

Anecdote: What You Don't Know Can Land You in a Foreign Jail

Our factory in Turkey had some ups and downs, and management was changed several times. I came in as an interim solution to add stability and to help define the skill sets needed for the next general manager. The factory leaders were being pushy. As an American, I was trying to better understand what they really wanted. In any event, they demanded higher pay, and when I basically said no, they decided to go on strike. I looked at this as a negotiation tactic and asked my secretary, Meryem, to come with me to make sure that there were no translation issues. My conversation with Meryem went something like this:

Meryem: Strike is illegal in Turkey.

Richard: Okay, so let's go talk with them, understand what they want, and tell them that strikes are illegal.

Meryem: No, you need to report the strike within eight hours.

Richard: Oh, so let's go talk with them and then we will report the strike.

Meryem: No, you can go to jail if the strike is not reported in time, and the police may not arrive for several hours, so you need to report the strike right now or risk going to jail.

I confirmed the need for urgency with the US Embassy.

Needless to say, I did report the strike. I also considered getting on the next airplane out of the country to avoid the potential of being arbitrarily put in jail.

Do not assume that the legal structures and approaches are the same everywhere! They are not the same, and the consequences for assuming and not knowing can be serious.

Headquarters

You started out with a good relationship at headquarters. It would be really silly to believe that the initial investment is all that is required.

If you are an American and the HQ is in the United States, there is a great chance that you want to return to the

HQ someday in a key position. The chances of you returning to HQ are slim if you have not maintained and nourished your relationships. As you did when you went to work for the company, you need to develop team relationships with people who may be interested in an international assignment and therefore can be part of your team at headquarters.

Just like forming relationships from HQ to the international groups, it is critical to maintain and grow your relationships at the home base.

Start by having a regular dialog and catch-up session with your current contacts. Every time you return to HQ, spend some time meeting everyone that you know and seeking introductions to new people in key positions. Do not forget the administrative and support people, since they often are the key that make the difference when you need a phone call answered (or returned) quickly.

There is one other key personal reason for maintaining and growing your relationships at HQ.

It is common for someone who is doing well in overseas posts to be considered an expert there. It is also common for HQ to leave that person and family in that area forever, without any thought that they might like to return to the United States.

Communication is a delicate art. You cannot repeat that you would like to return to the United States every time you speak with an executive from HQ. That would result in someone worrying that you were not doing well in your current assignment.

There is often a belief that general management in another country, particularly in developing nations, is easier than similar posts in the home country.

An executive asked me if running the $50 million operation in Morocco would be similar to running a $5 million operation in the United States. I said no. It is not even close when you consider languages, culture, different banking relationships, dealing with export and import changes, local security, concern for all expatriate families, and many other things that would never be required in a home-country operation (except for CEO of the parent company). My view is that it is more like managing an operation twice that size ($100 million) in the United States.

Reentry to the home country is eventually an issue. I could not cover all that is required to make reentry successful for the returning executive and family. The most I can say is that HQ rarely understands that a new post requires just as much support and facilitation as the first international assignment.

Review for Problem Solving and Culture

- There are basic differences in the approach to problem solving by culture.
- Solutions to the problems are usually similar.
- Exposure to other cultures is critical for a global business career.
- The most important aspect of reaching a solution to a problem in a multicultural environment is the process.

Active listening is critical for success.

"The only source of knowledge is experience"

—Albert Einstein

Chapter 6
Travel Safety, Security and Protection

Travel is fun sometimes. When it is a key part of your job, it requires some serious planning and thought.

I traveled with a very smart friend through a number of countries on my first assignment. I noticed that he always gave the people at the front desk of the hotel ten dollars each (usually three or four people) when we checked in. I also noticed that he gave small gifts or cash to airline people at the airports. I started paying more attention and watched similar actions for concierge personnel, the maître d' at restaurants, customs officials, immigration personnel, floor housekeepers at the hotels, and others. These were not bribes. He asked for their names, and each time as the relationship grew, he talked about their families, children, grandchildren, and he introduced me into these relationships as a friend and colleague.

My curiosity could not be contained. When I asked him why he did this, he said it is important that these people recognize you and believe that you are a good person. There may come a time when the hotel is overbooked, or the flight oversold, or a security breach occurs, but when they see your name or see you in person, they will remember your thoughtfulness and give you preference over others. This is ethical in all cultures.

If your passport has only six months to go before expiration, be aware that some countries require more than six months, and you could be denied entry. It is much nicer to have someone simply say, "You know that we are expected to deny entry to anyone without more than six months left on their passport. However, since we know you, please enter, and please update your passport before you return again."

Security is also an issue. If you are recognized as a regular guest, frequent flyer, or frequent visitor through immigration, you will be kept informed of security and like issues. This has value much greater than the money or the friendly smile for the people that work in areas that you frequent.

I moved on to my next assignment and began many long trips around the world with my next post. I also made a habit of doing the same thing that I had learned from my first assignment.

Anecdote: A Cost–Benefit Analysis of a Three-Dollar Bracelet

I found some silver bracelets in Bali that cost roughly three dollars each and purchased a hundred of them. I gave them out to key airline desk agents and front desk personnel. I cannot tell you how many times that investment was repaid.

Every time I visited a hotel or airport, the ladies would be wearing their bracelets and would greet me with a smile and say, "Good to see you again, Mr. Lindenmuth."

One time I found that a hotel was completely booked due to a government meeting. It was 11:00 p.m. when I arrived from the airport, and no other hotels were close or available. There was a crowd at the front desk (many had arrived on the same airplane), and it was clear that nothing could be done. A woman at the front desk nodded her head toward the hotel restaurant. I went in and found that she arrived moments later with good news. She had seen me arrive and arranged with the owner of the large store that was part of the first floor in the hotel to allow me to spend the night on the couch in the store. The owner locked me in at midnight and was there just after morning prayers to open the door. I did this for two days. I purchased a rug that the owner of the store recommended, and I thanked everyone for taking care of me.

Anecdote: Personal Security

Security in airports is not always as it is in the United States and Europe. The airports in one of the countries that I traveled to frequently would experience last-minute changes to flights or security patterns. I provided the airlines ladies and security people with gifts, tips, and occasionally just conversation about family, sports, or other topics of interest. The result was that if I arrived running for a flight, I could jump to the front of the line. It is important to be respectful and to not abuse these relationships.

One time as I was moving toward the front of the line, I noticed an American family that I knew waiting in line for the same flight. The gate was closing, so they would clearly miss the flight. I asked them to follow me, and I took them around the security scanners and handed my passport (and the others') to the chief security officer on duty. He smiled and said that he would see me next week and we all made the airplane.

Another time I had to abandon my apartment in Beirut during some heavy military fighting. I basically left everything behind except for family photographs. When my household goods were shipped to my new home in Greece, they included things that would not have been shipped in the United States. One of these things was a telephone that had been hardwired into the wall in the apartment. It was an Arabic phone and of no use outside of Lebanon. I decided that the next time that I went back to Beirut, I would simply take it with me and return it to the landlord.

Well, I put it in my briefcase and headed off to Beirut only to find that the ceasefire had been broken and that the airport was closed. Okay, this kind of thing happens. I just headed to my next destination, which was Algiers. This happened on the same day that the Saudi King was assassinated, and security in all airports was at the top levels.

When I arrived and went through immigration, the security officer that checked my bags opened my briefcase and saw the telephone (remember, this is before cell phones). He asked me about the telephone and I joked that you never can tell when you are going to get a call. His response was, "No, you can tap telephone lines. You are a spy." I was immediately taken into custody. Good news: Two of the airport ladies that I had given bracelets to in prior visits came up and asked what was going on. I simply asked them to tell the guards that I was really a good guy and not a dangerous spy. They had a long conversation with the guards, everyone smiled, and I was put on the next airplane out of the country (Air France to Marseilles) with an armed escort.

Once they sat me in first class and took the handcuffs off, I was thankful for the small bracelets. Interestingly, no one on the airplane talked to me for the entire trip to Marseilles. I am sure with the handcuffs and armed escort, they were sure that I was an evil person!

There are more everyday legal issues that should be considered as well.

I no longer drive a car in any country outside of the United States or Europe. Cars with drivers are available at reasonable rates. Using one eliminates the exposure to local laws and practices that Americans would never even consider.

Knowing that you should not drive an automobile in many countries can also enhance security. Rental car companies may be happy to rent you a vehicle whereupon everything seems to be just like it is back home. That is not the case.

In one country, an older American couple was traveling on a long-anticipated retirement trip. There was a car accident involving a number of automobiles, and they were wedged in between cars with no damage to them or their vehicle. There was a fatality, and they noticed that everyone else ran away quickly. They waited until the police arrived so that they could tell what they saw occur, as would be expected in the United States and many other countries. Unexpectedly, they were arrested and taken to jail where they stayed for a significant time as the local US Counsel explained that they had to "exhaust local remedies" (in other words, wait for the local authorities to do their jobs). Even though they did not do anything, the US Counsel could not help them.

Anecdote: The Cost of Not Knowing

A local I knew bought his son a new car in a country where I would not drive. A month later, his son hit a man on a road with no streetlights. The man was thrown up on the car, went through the windshield on the passenger side, and landed on the passenger seat, dead.

I knew local law required that anyone charged with something like this had to go to jail. I asked the father to tell me the full story. His serious and interesting response was that I was right, and that someone had to be charged. He met with the family of the now deceased man and agreed to pay them for their loss. In return, the deceased was charged with "breaking and entering" the vehicle, and no other charges were filed.

The best lesson is to think twice and be well informed about local laws prior to driving an automobile anywhere outside of the United States, Canada, and Western Europe.

There are other lessons. In the United States and Western Europe, we are taught to respect authority. Frequently, this authority is authenticated just by the fact that the person is wearing a uniform, such as a policeman, fireman, or military personnel with weapons. This automatic respect for authority should be replaced with questions and curiosity at the very least when you are in another country. It is not uncommon for people to take advantage of Westerners' knee-jerk respect for signs of authority.

Anecdote: Leave Your Weapons on the Sofa, Please

In the Middle East, I arrived at my office one morning to have my secretary inform me that armed men were inside. I asked her what they wanted, and her only response was, "They have guns, so I let them in." I had to think for a moment on this one. If they had meant harm, it would already have been done. They did not even know my name.

In the Middle East, it is important to follow cultural hospitality guidelines. I went into the office, and everyone politely stood up. I smiled and said that I was sorry that I was not there when they arrived to offer them the proper hospitality. I then asked if they would mind exiting my office so that I could properly invite them in. They thought this was a bit curious, but they all exited the office. I then said, "Please allow me to invite you into my office," and as they started in I said, "Please put your weapons on the couch," which they promptly did. I then invited them for coffee, and when the proper friendly social conversations were over, I asked what I could do for them. They asked for a donation to the Popular Liberation Front to help refuges in the camps. I said that as an American company we were not allowed to give money, but that I would be able to give some sewing machines and a refrigerator. They were delighted, and as they left I suggested that if they want to return, please send just one representative without weapons.

Anecdote: Prevalence of Weapons

I was in Beirut during the civil strife, in the back seat of a car with my professional Palestinian driver at the wheel. We were practically the only car on the road since there had been fighting in various locations around the city all morning. We were going slowly and just stopped our car at a traffic light. A jeep filled with armed men stopped opposite us at the same light. It was one of those lights that just seemed to go on being red forever. I was going to suggest that we just go right through it since no other cars were visible.

Just then the passenger in the front of the jeep reached out with an AK-47 and shot the traffic light to pieces. I initially ducked down, but once I determined the target was the red light we all waved to one another and went our way! I'm sorry I didn't have a video-capable smartphone at the time. Every time I'm stuck at a long red light, I remember that adventure.

Anecdote: Open Up, It's the Police

In another case in West Africa, I had just gotten to sleep when the sound of gun butts hitting my hotel door awakened me. I went to the door and asked who was there. The response was: "The police." I asked what they wanted, and they asked me to open the door. I said that they should go down to the front desk and talk to the manager, Mr. Marcus, and that if he believed it was important, he would call my room and let me know. They thought for a moment and then said that they were collecting for the PLM (Popular Liberation Movement). I laughed and said that I already contributed and they went away.

In this case, I had a different thought. I opened the door and suggested that the guy in 303 really admired the PLM. A senior executive that always asked me to guide him when he traveled to Africa had annoyed me by constantly insisting on breakfast meetings at 6:00 a.m. In Africa, where air conditioning was not always available, it was a solid practice to go to bed later, sleep later, and go to work just when the day warmed up. After a week of travel, I was tired, and my humor overruled my usual good judgment.

The next morning, at the 6:00 a.m. breakfast meeting, my New York colleague was abnormally late. When he did arrive, he looked as though he had not slept all night. When I asked what happened he said, "The police came to my room last night asking for donations." I said that I hoped he had followed my directions and never let anyone, including the police or military, in his room.

He responded, "It was the police, so I opened the door." I said, gosh, I hope that you didn't give them anything. Basically, he said that they had guns and he gave them all his cash, roughly $1200, and traveler's checks. Wow! I told him that we could easily get the travelers checks back and suggested that he had given them enough cash for a year's salary in this country. Thinking out loud, I said that they were probably pretty happy guys. He responded that they ordered room service and played cards in his room all night. I never did have the nerve to tell him how they found his room. I don't think he ever would have forgiven me!

When you are on a foreign assignment, you are not in your home country or culture. Do not open your hotel door just because someone claims to be the police. Also, remember those small gifts and cash given to front desk personnel. This is extra insurance to keep from being annoyed—or worse.

Anecdote: Confidence is Everything

I was in the Ivory Coast at one of the big marketplaces near the downtown hotel district. I had just had a great morning meeting with my company team, so I thought that I would go for a walk with a camera and take some pictures of the colorful outfits seen in the market. While I was there, a police team came in to perform what they call *chasé les rats*—basically, "chase the rats." This refers to young children who come to the market to steal carvings and other things that they then put on a blanket and present in front of the hotels for tourists. I was standing there watching when a police officer came to me, grabbed me by the arm, led me to a paddy wagon almost filled with young "rats," and accused me of taking unauthorized pictures of police proceedings. It took me a moment to compose myself while looking at the amazed faces of my young colleagues in the paddy wagon. When the next policeman opened the door (and looked equally amazed to see me), I pushed my way out, pointed my finger at his nose, and said to him, "Get your commanding officer here right away," which he did. I then opened the camera and took out the film, exposing all of it, and said that now there can be no case for unauthorized photos and that I had no intention of remaining in a place where they treat business executives in that manner. I walked off, somewhat surprised that they did not come after me. I also lost a full day of colorful pictures and was careful from that point on if I even carried a camera!

Once in a while you have a cultural experience that is circumstantial. This is something all of us might like to do at some point but will never get the chance.

Today there are some extra precautions to consider. Traveling with your smartphone, laptop, iPad, and using public or even hotel Wi-Fi is considered normal. Cybercrime is rampant anywhere. However, it is more prevalent in some current business destinations. China is one in particular that requires some caution.

It is not uncommon to arrive in a country and have someone ask to inspect your laptop as you pass through immigration.

It is also not uncommon to have them take your laptop into another room and copy the hard drive! There are variations on what is done with this information.

In some areas, the governments want to follow you and track your communications. In other areas, the info is sold or given to "friends." Cybercrime is a major issue.

There is no particular remedy for these cyber issues. I prefer to use a one-time telephone or one that I reserve for travel to these adventurous locations so that I am sure no personal or company info of any value is available for the taking. The same is true of a laptop, although today an iPad for travel (with no business or personal data) makes a great deal of sense.

I also prefer to use international hotels that have Internet access in their business centers for routine emails and communications, using only the hotel computers.

Anecdote: English Only

Once I placed a reservation for a telephone call to the United States from Egypt. I was asked for the telephone number to be called and was eventually given a date and time (four days to be able to make the call) and asked for the language to be spoken on the call, to which I responded English. When I placed the call, the secretary of the executive I was calling (a charming French lady) began a quick conversation while we were waiting for the boss to get on the line. The conversation was in French, and after not much more than *"Bon jour, tu vas bien?"* a male voice came on the line and said, in a commanding manner, "English only." I never again questioned whether someone might be listening in on my phone conversations.

"An ounce of prevention" is a saying that has been valid for a long time. When we leave our comfortable culture, we need to consider everything. We routinely get vaccinated for yellow fever or take malaria medication, depending on where our travels take us. We need to consider similar precautions for our digital protection.

These precautions are being upgraded regularly. Encryption software and other programs can be installed easily today. Always make sure you have copies in the cloud or at the home office for backup.

Richard Lindenmuth

"Always try to associate yourself with and learn as much as you can from those who know more than you do, who do better than you, who see more clearly than you"
—Dwight D. Eisenhower

CHAPTER 7
A Local Guide

When we leave home base and the culture and security that we believe is universal, there are times when we need someone to show us and to keep us on the correct path. Language translation is sometimes the only thing that we consider, since we recognize that we do not understand even common words in other languages.

Two comments: First, how do you know that the translator is actually saying exactly what you said? Make sure that the translator is from a reputable source, such as your local office (not the hotel, unless you are simply going shopping). Second, the language is only one consideration when laws, regulations, local customs, and basically everything is different from back home. You need a guide to assure that you avoid basic but troublesome mistakes.

Richard Lindenmuth

Anecdote: Not Everything Needs Translation

An American was dealing with a union issue in Italy and called a meeting with the union officials to negotiate a resolution. First, he simply chose a young, attractive lady from the hotel to act as his translator. The meeting began, and after polite introductions were made, the American began a half-hour dissertation on his demands. The "translator" had no real experience and did not interrupt the American to allow flowing translation. She also had no way to remember the entire dissertation. A good translator will stop you every few sentences so they are sure they remember everything and have the translation correct.

The good and bad news was that as the American ended his dissertation by telling everyone that he expected his demands to be met immediately, he added to the translator, "I hope these imbeciles understand how stupid they are acting." As the translator started to make a comment, the union leader jumped up on the conference table, walked from the other end up to the American, looked down, and (with a little more colorful language than I use here) said: "Some of us actually went to university and speak reasonable English. None of us are imbeciles. I suggest that you go back to where you come from and permit someone with more respect and intelligence to handle these discussions!"

The American left on the next airplane to New York and made me swear that I would never tell anyone what just happened. He was clearly embarrassed.

Two observations are necessary. First, do not assume that everyone in a discussion has no grasp of your native language. Second, it takes skill to speak in small bites to allow the translators to do their job. A good translation requires as much skill and dedication from you as it does your translator. It is wise to meet with your translator before an important meeting to set up guidelines for both of you.

Translation is an art. Simultaneous translation such as that used in the United Nations is rare (translators often have a written copy of the speech as well). It takes time and effort to learn how to benefit from a translator. If you speak two or three sentences at a time and then wait for translation, it provides the translator time to do it correctly, and it also allows you to watch the reaction from your audience carefully.

If you are speaking about technical issues, or areas where a great deal of detail and perhaps specialized vocabulary is required, a translator with some specific knowledge and experience is necessary. Most important, some rehearsal and time for practice is required.

You would not go on safari without a guide. When you are doing business in a local culture, there may be no wild animals ready to attack. However, you can avoid dangerous traps by using a competent guide.

Cultural Business Guides

Guides can come in many forms. An example of this is when my company decided to build a factory in Indonesia. I was asked to search in an area near convenient transportation for a parcel of land that would accommodate our current needs and also allow us to grow in the future.

I spent several days just looking for the appropriate office or person to help me with this mission. Ultimately, I found a recommended local businessman who became our strategic partner. He provided someone to do some basic research with our guidelines and return with some specific locations to be considered. This is not something that can be done in a day or two, even in the United States.

There were lots of discussions and false starts, but two weeks later we agreed on two potential properties. I secured headquarters' approval to move ahead. I fully expected to deal with the property owner to negotiate a reasonable price. Wow, was I wrong!

The guidance of the local strategic partner eventually had me sitting in the middle of the acreage with the sort-of equivalent of a local government representative (basically a county clerk with all of the land registration documents in a handwritten book) with a small table and a suitcase filled with local currency. Both the local strategic partner and the local government representative acted as guides to me throughout this process. The guides greeted each parcel holder as a friend or relative and often told me "This parcel was farmed by his great-grandfather" or "He was born right here on this parcel." Every single person we met in this case was male.

People lined up, and the government representative validated their identification documents as well as the particular parcel that they or their families owned. Some parcels were not much bigger than a small American backyard or a British garden. Each person signed a government document selling his or her land (most with the equivalent of an X), which was witnessed and validated by the government representative. Prices varied with the size of the lot and the stature of the family that owned it, but all of the prices were reasonable when translated into US dollars. Some of the parcels cost the equivalent of less than USD 500.

The last two individuals, with parcels almost in the middle of the location, held out and wanted almost twice as much as everyone else had received. The local government representative was a terrific guide. He told me to look very serious and perhaps seem to consider saying no to the transaction. He and I had a brief discussion about local traditions (I was still looking very serious) and how it was important to respect these particular community leaders. He then talked for a considerable amount of time with the two leaders. Next he turned to me and basically told me to smile and be positive.

Our deal was then done with all of the signatures (Xs) confirmed and validated by the government representative, and with what seemed like at least one hundred postage-like stamps attached, I received confirmation that we owned the property.

It still took months to obtain all of the local construction, right-of-way, and other approvals before the initial groundbreaking ceremony could take place.

Without the guidance of both the local partner and the government official, I would have never been able to navigate buying all of those parcels. Not only that, the guide saved me lots of money by explaining the culture and how I should react when they asked for twice the amount that was fair.

> "Once you have visited foreign shores
> you can ne'er go home again."
> —Nathanial Hawthorne

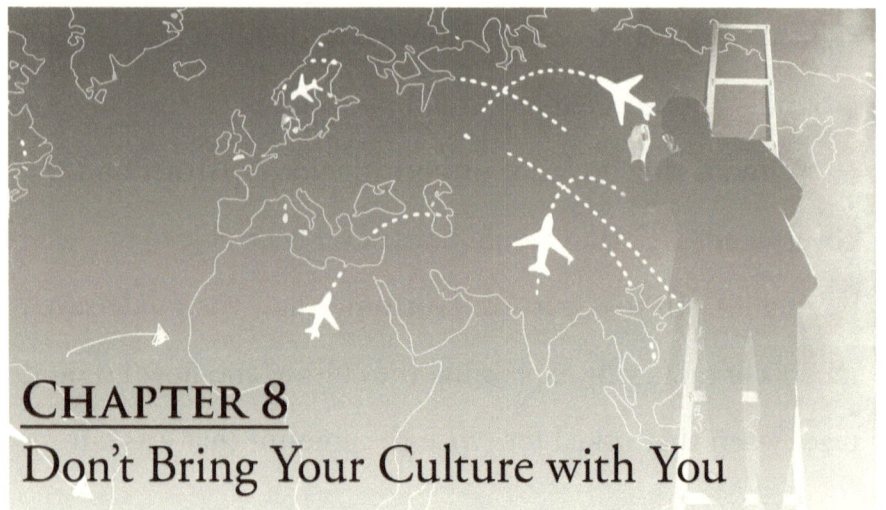

Chapter 8
Don't Bring Your Culture with You

Once you have traveled and been immersed in other cultures, you develop an appreciation for the way things are done outside of your home culture. One of my children interpreted this as follows: "For the first six months, you miss hamburgers and Sponge Bob Square Pants, but then you begin to enjoy couscous and tangerines and don't miss television at all."

An interesting example of culture and expectation happened in my office in Hong Kong. Our HR director from New York visited as part of her international familiarization tour. We gave her an operational tour and respected the jet lag factor. We showed her the office and then took a ferryboat to visit the factory. Basically it was a business sightseeing tour.

One the third day, we spent a great deal of time going over written policies (all were in Chinese and English). According to local regulations, some of the safety regulations were posted for everyone to see. We worked hard from 7:30 a.m. and realized at 1:00 p.m. we had not taken time for lunch. I gave her a menu and asked what she would like. I suggested dim sum and she agreed. I then asked my admin to "just make me an omelet" as well.

I had a meeting during the mid-afternoon, and when I returned, my secretary informed me that the HR executive had asked for a meeting with all the admin and support people, and that during that meeting she informed them that this is an American company, and that they did not have to make coffee or omelets as part of their job. I did not know what to say, but before I could say anything, the admin group said collectively, "She really doesn't know how things work here in Hong Kong, does she?" While she may have been trying to look out for the well-being of the employees, in reality, she insulted them in addition to leaving the impression that she was no expert in human relations by not understanding their culture. Of course, from a purely American culture perspective from someone who had never been outside of the United States, my asking the admin to make an omelet was sexist and would never happen in the United States.

It is important to know that you do not take your culture or HQ policies with you when you travel.

Anecdote: WAWA (West Africa Wins Again)

Sometimes things happen so often in a particular area that when talking with people who have similar "regional" experience, broad statements can be made. One example of WAWA happened in Ghana.

I was traveling to Lagos, Nigeria, and I arrived early at the airport in Ghana just in case there were any issues with the flight. As I approached the ticket counter for the flight to Lagos, I saw a number of people that I knew line up behind me.

I said, "Good morning. I'm on flight 689 to Nigeria."

The ticket counter supervisor announced, "Oh, I am sorry, flight 689 for today has been delayed until tomorrow morning."

The line behind me expressed concern. However, having some experience with these matters, I said, "Oh, what about flight 689 from yesterday?"

The response was, "Sure, flight 689 from yesterday will

be leaving on time today." I had no trouble getting a seat on flight 689 from yesterday!

Anecdote: Hospitality Is Not about Paying the Bill

We were invited to a wonderful geisha house for dinner and karaoke in Tokyo. My colleague was a board member of my company and had never traveled outside of the United States. We had been dinner, luncheon, and travel guests for eight days, and this was dinner on the last evening. My colleague said, "Dick, let me pick up the bill. They have been paying for everything since we arrived."

My response was, "You will cause a serious problem. We will pay when they visit us in the United States, but I will get you a copy of the bill so that you can understand that this would not fit on an American company's expense account."

The host company chairman paid for dinner, and after considerable bowing and thank-yous (*arrigato gozimus*, etc.), I gave my colleague a copy of the bill for dinner for six, plus karaoke and unlimited drinks, and a nice lady sitting next to each of us to make sure that our glasses were full and that there were no awkward lapses in the conversation. When he first did the math, he came up with $850 for the total. When I showed him that he dropped a zero and that the charge was $8500, his first comment was, "That would be a week of dinners in Louisville."

It is truly a challenge to overcome the feeling or need to bring your culture with you, and only local guides and personal experience can help you to overcome this compulsion.

"A traveler without observation is a bird without wings."
—Moslih Eddin Saadi

CHAPTER 9
Financial Statements

It is always a headquarters requirement to have financial statements structured and formatted in the shape that is normal and expected from the home country accounting and financial requirements. It is not expected to have all home country practices translated and installed in global operations.

One interesting example came with a visitor from New York. He said that he was here to assess our overhead structure. As his review progressed, one of his comments was that "although you have a sizeable office, you have way too many messengers and coffee makers." If I had disagreed with his observation, we would have had an argument that would extend to HQ. I suggested that we did have a large number of people acting as messengers and coffee servers, but that I thought it was important for him to continue his assessment by staying with one of the messenger–coffee makers for an entire day.

When we arrived at the office the next day, I introduced Achmed, who served Turkish coffee, *masbut* (medium sweet), to our visitor. I let Achmed know that he would have a companion for the day. I knew what his schedule was but did not let on to our visitor from headquarters that he was in for an interesting day.

Late that afternoon, Achmed returned with an exhausted and disgusted visitor. He said that he had just spent the entire day in the local government offices with Achmed. They had been politely ushered into a waiting room where, after forty-five minutes, they had a brief discussion with someone who then provided a stamp on a document. Next they went to another building with that document and waited another hour before a signature and a block of tax stamp was attached to the document. They then had a quick lunch and returned to the same building they had originally visited, in the same waiting room where, after an hour, Achmed made a cash payment and received a receipt.

I explained to our visitor that Achmed was simply going

through the process of paying our water bill. I also explained that several of the other messengers were doing similar tasks for electric and other bills, and that each of the foreign residents had similar bills for their apartments, schools, automobiles, and so on. It didn't take our visitor long to understand that if each one of us had to stand in line to pay our normal bills in cash, nothing would ever get done in the office. And he left with a new appreciation for Turkish coffee.

Financial statements are important to understand. It is common for some countries to require only an opening balance and a closing balance for a year. Morocco (for example) is a French-speaking country with strong business influence from France and therefore a base accounting system that follows French accounting rules. If you are working for an American firm with US GAAP accounting, the accounts need to be able to respond to those requirements. Since the local accounting system is French and auditors understand the French system, the accounts need to be correct in the French system. Of course, you also have to be in sync with the local government regulations. Sounds really challenging!

Today, with computers and spreadsheets, it's actually pretty easy. Large international company and country requirements are not that different. One example in French versus US accounting is the balance sheet treatment of "plus value" (French) and "goodwill" (US).

All of these small differences can be done correctly, first in the country of origin, and then be adjusted for the parent company's requirements. Managerial accounting—basically taking the performance data and presenting it in a format that is easy to understand by local management and parent company directors—is equally straightforward.

Tools such as Excel and Smartsheet provide many ways to facilitate a company standard approach across all accounting systems and cultures.

> "It must be, I thought, one of the race's most persistent hallucinations to trust that 'it can't happen here'—that one's own time and place is beyond cataclysm."
> —John Windham, The Day of the Triffids

CHAPTER 10
Review

Working for a multinational company provides you with wonderful opportunities for travel and for personal and professional growth. Yet it can be quite challenging to get started in an international position because you often need international experience to get a job overseas. One of the best ways to get around this is to first work in the HQ in your native land. While there you should focus on making great connections and developing strong relationships with members both at the HQ and on international teams. Strong relationships with members at HQ will help you immeasurably when you do get your job overseas because you will have the support of HQ. It can also be wise to get financial experience first since you can move from finance to other industries, but it is difficult to go into finance from other specialties.

Make sure that you spend time studying everything there is to know about the international operations you want to be a part of. When the team you are interested in comes to HQ for a review or meetings, ask if you can sit in and observe. Take notes and try to identify a subject, risk, concern, or opportunity that you could help solve. Reach out to the team after the meeting to share your thoughts. You should also take this time to express your interest in joining the team to a junior team member. Invite that person out for a drink at a local hotspot to build a better relationship between the two of you. Make sure you follow up with the team afterward though email. "Out of sight, out of mind" is true in every culture.

Learning languages is also important to international success. Language is the path to understanding the culture, values, and social etiquette. You don't need to be fluent in every language, but you should spend some time studying the language of the country you want to work in.

Remember that where you work on an international assignment is not home, and there will be things that your new culture does that will seem odd or even wrong. By all means find a good guide to help you navigate these issues.

Learning how different cultures solve problems and make decisions is key to your success as a manager. It is important to learn meeting etiquette and techniques that the culture you are working in uses to solve problems. Observation and active listening are *essential* to doing this!

While working abroad, it is essential to stay in contact with HQ and keep the relationships you made while working there strong. This is especially important if you ever wish to move back to working at HQ.

Traveling can be fun, or it can be long and tedious. One way to make it much more enjoyable is to greet people by name and give small gifts to the workers in places you frequent. This can pay huge dividends in your travels.

It is also wise to be cautious when traveling. Cybercrime is rampant in many places. Make sure you have secure passwords on both your laptop and phone. It can be smart to get a prepaid phone while you are abroad to minimize the risk of becoming a victim of cybercrime.

Getting a good local guide is also a key to your success and safety while working abroad. Guides will help you avoid costly or dangerous pitfalls and to navigate an unknown land and culture.

Overall, working abroad as a manager or executive has a ton of amazing benefits. You get to experience wonderful places and cultures, and you get to learn more about the inner workings of your company. Immersing yourself in other cultures will help your brain expand and see things from different perspectives, which will help you in future problem solving. While it can be challenging to secure your first international job, the benefits you will reap far outweigh the challenges!

> "Life is 10 percent what happens to me and 90 percent of how I react to it."
> —Charles Swindoll

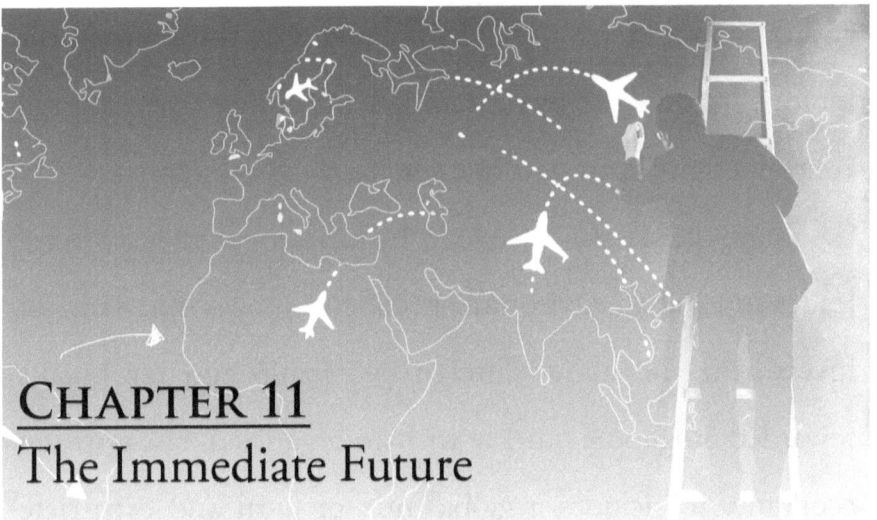

CHAPTER 11
The Immediate Future

The future is filled with opportunities for global economic development. International executives will be the architects of the new global economy!

Technology is changing, and ADC (Advanced Digital Connectivity), including high-speed (10 Gbps) connectivity are becoming more important for economic development and selecting sites for manufacturing and office locations for multinational companies. International executives will be key to developing the global architecture that connects economies to the global marketplace of the future.

It is easy to see the areas that are ready for next steps. Eastern Europe, Hungary, Romania, Croatia, Latvia, Estonia, Moldavia, Czechoslovakia, the Philippines, Thailand, and Malaysia all come to mind. All of these countries have government leadership problems along with the requirement for forward thinking by the families and groups that currently control a significant part of each country's economy.

Singapore is an excellent historical example. Strong leadership and an environment that encourages international investment and allows foreign ownership and tax breaks rewarded Singapore quickly with an organized, fast-growing economy. It includes a global mix of local and expatriate investors and executives.

One last observation: Singapore did not have large legacy infrastructure (telecom) investments to protect. Therefore modern infrastructure developed quickly to support global investments.

Local families that controlled a great part of the economy did not lose control and have diminished investment values when new global investors arrived. Actually, local businesses grew faster than ever, providing the supply chain for global investors as well as taking advantage of opportunities that never would have appeared without global investments.

The Philippines, too, is a wonderful example. The Philippines has great geographic location for the Asia markets. It has the advantage of having English as its second language along with Tagalog, and it even has the largest Wharton (University of Pennsylvania) alumni club outside of the United States.

The foremost driver of the opportunities in these countries, along with their individual markets, geography, and languages, is technology. The advanced digital infrastructure has the ability to connect all of these countries to global markets, customers, suppliers, partners, and investors, and to level the playing field with all global competitors large and small.

Just as it was in Singapore years ago, the opportunity exists for these countries today to leapfrog to the latest technological infrastructure. An entire text could be written about the Advanced Digital Opportunity. But to capsulize, economic development has never happened without "dial tone." In the future, an economy that is not connected electronically to the digital global economy will be at a severe handicap.

The global connection starts with a broadband infrastructure that permits high-speed (at least 10 Gbps) of connectivity. This challenge includes the United States.

In 1964, 4 kilobytes of memory took up 64 cubic feet and cost $164. Today 4 kilobytes of memory is smaller than your fingernail and costs pennies. Today we expect to have 128 gigabytes available on our smartphones!

Broadband infrastructure is not about telephone or cable TV. It is about having a digital pipeline to the global economy. It does require collaboration between current telecom, energy, water, and other utilities and government and local economic leadership.

In the 1940s in the United States, rural residents went into town to make long distance telephone calls. There were not enough phone subscribers to make financial sense for the large telecom companies to expand their infrastructures into lightly populated areas. Municipalities got involved, and the development of rural telephone and energy co-ops evolved to provide coverage and connectivity.

Today we have broadband, fiber optics (Google and others), wireless, and other pipes. When you can get Netflix, NFL football, and anything else that you might want on the Internet, paying for a cable modem and cable TV has become an antique practice.

Available now are school courses; hospital programs to monitor diabetic patients over the net rather than have them visit doctors for a simple update; farmers who use the net to have the local university measure soil, fertilizer, and water contents; and energy smart grids that permit digital households to communicate with digital thermostats and security systems across the net.

In the United States, we have legacy infrastructures, major utilities, telecom, cable, and other companies that have interests in protecting existing systems and investments. This does not mean that the Philippines and other countries do not have some legacy systems. But we have examples in Seoul, South Korea, where the government owns many of the antennae and has worked with the local telephone companies to provide high-speed Internet connections for less than thirty dollars per month. In the United States Sandy, Oregon, decided to invest in high-speed Internet connectivity as a town, and they already have enough subscribers to make their investment commercially viable. They have also experienced economic growth and development that would not have occurred without this investment.

As the global marketplace becomes more interconnected and reliant on new technology to survive and thrive, individuals with a strong concept of how best to use these new technologies will be sought even more than international executives. While millennials still have a lack of professional experience, their inherent understanding of the new connected world will become increasingly important and valued in coming years. In fact, you are already starting to see baby boomers with immense business knowledge partnering with millennials who have strong technical knowledge in mutually beneficial relationships. With many Third World countries investing in legacy infrastructure, the new world of international executives will come rushing in. It is truly a landscape of opportunity for those who want to travel, learn, and embrace other cultures, all while helping these new economies develop and prosper.

www.ingramcontent.com/pod-product-compliance
Lightning Source LLC
Chambersburg PA
CBHW030855180526
45163CB00004B/1582